SILLY MEASUREMENTS

How Many Kittens Could Ride a Shark?

CREATIVE WAYS TO LOOK AT LENGTH

by Clara Cella

PEBBLE
a capstone imprint

T0084484

How many
kittens
could ride a shark,
thrilling the
guests at the
sea life park?

Printed and bound in the USA. PO#

18
kittens!

MOO! says
the **cow**.
Here's a stumper:
How long is a bus,
from bumper
to bumper?

4 cows
long!
STOP

EMERGENCY EXIT

How many toy **planes**, end to end, match the wings of *this* feathered friend?

7 toy planes!

How long is
an **otter**?
Do you know?

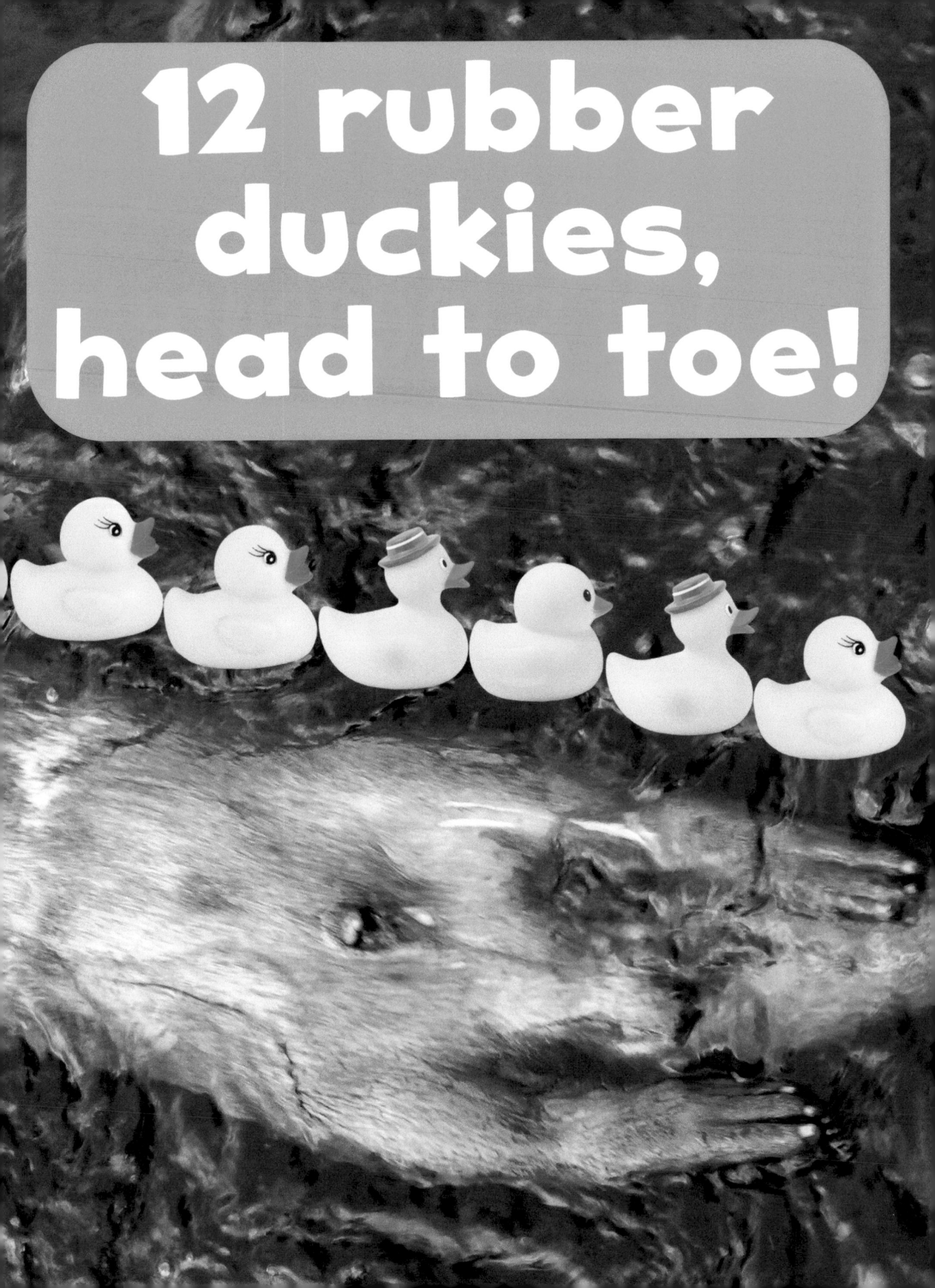
12 rubber
duckies,
head to toe!

Let's measure this **tail**, 1-2-3! How many gumballs would it be?

20
gumballs!

Here's an idea that sounds a bit weird: Use a **bird** to measure a beard!

This beard is 3 birds long!

Measuring a **crayon** is a piece of cake! How many inchworms would it take?

4
inchworms!

Is this statement a lie or a truth? A **mouse** is as long as a lion's tooth.

TRUTH!

LOOK FOR OTHER BOOKS IN THE SERIES:

Pebble Sprout is published by Pebble, an imprint of Capstone.
1710 Roe Crest Drive, North Mankato, Minnesota 56003
www.capstonepub.com

Copyright © 2020 by Capstone. All rights reserved. No part of this publication may be reproduced in whole or in part, or stored in a retrieval system, or transmitted in any form or by any means, electronic, mechanical, photocopying, recording, or otherwise, without written permission of the publisher.

Library of Congress Cataloging-in-Publication Data

Names; Cella, Clara, author.
Title; How many kittens could ride a shark? ; creative ways to look at length / by Clara Cella.
Description; North Mankato, Minnesota; Pebble, [2020] | Series; Silly measurements | Audience; Ages 4-6 | Audience; Grades K-1 | Summary;Introduce pre-readers to the math concept of length with eight goofy, non-standard measuring units, including kittens, toy airplanes, and gumballs. Delightful composite photos and a sprinkling of text illustrate the length of a shark, a lemur tail, a crayon, and more;— Provided by publisher.
Identifiers; LCCN 2019043573 (print) | LCCN 2019043574 (ebook)
ISBN 9781977113238 (hardcover) | ISBN 9781977120106 (paperback) | ISBN 9781977113276 (ebook pdf)
Subjects; LCSH; Length measurement—Juvenile literature.
Classification; LCC QC102 .C45 2020 (print) | LCC QC102 (ebook) | DDC 530.8—dc23
LC record available at https;//lccn.loc.gov/2019043573 LC ebook record available at https;//lccn.loc.gov/2019043574

Image Credits

Shutterstock: 5 Second Studio, 4 (gray kitten), 5, almond, 20–21 (lemur), Anest, 28 (stretched inchworm), 29, Anna Utekhina, cover (cat's paws), 1, Charles Brutlag, 23, 24 (finch), 25 (finches), CLS Digital Arts, 29 (inchworm), ConstantinosZ, 12 (red, white, and blue toy plane), cynoclub, 4 (Bengal kitten), 5, Dmitry Kalinovsky, 4 (dark orange tabby kitten), 5, Dx09, 9 (front left), Eric Isselee, 3, 8 (front left and right), 9 (front right), 11, 30, 31 (mouse), Ewa Studio, 4 (orange tabby kitten), 5, GrashAlex, 12 (red toy plane), 13, GrigoryL, 4 (striped kitten), 5, Jay Bo, 31 (lion), Kitch Bain, 20 (gumballs), 21, Luis_Vazquez, 28–29 (crayons), Lukas Walter, 4–5 (shark), M Kunz, 7, Mtsaride, 27, Nerthuz, cover (top), back cover, Picsfive, 16 (rubber duck with eyelashes), 17, Randy van Domselaar, 15, ReaLiia, 12 (blue toy plane), 13, Sebastian Reinholdtsen, 16–17 (otter), sebra, 24–25 (bearded face), Sergey Uryadnikov, 12–13 (eagle), silky, 8–9 (bus), Sittirak Jadlit, 16 (plain rubber duck), 17, Tony Campbell, 4 (white and gray tabby kittens), 5, tratong, 19, Tsekhmister, 16 (rubber duck with blue hat), 17, Yuliia Sonsedska, cover (cat), 1

Editorial Credits

Editor: Jill Kalz; Designer: Ted Williams; Media Researcher: Svetlana Zhurkin; Production Specialist: Katy LaVigne

Printed in the United States 5183